dabble lab

AMAZING MAGIC TRICKS

PRESTO CHANGO!

TRICKS FOR SKILLED MAGICIANS

4D™

A MAGICAL AUGMENTED
READING
EXPERIENCE

• • • BY NORM BARNHART • • •

CAPSTONE PRESS
a capstone imprint

Dabble Lab is published by
Capstone Press, A Capstone Imprint
1710 Roe Crest Drive
North Mankato, Minnesota 56003
www.mycapstone.com

Library of Congress Cataloging-in-Publication Data
Names: Barnhart, Norm, author.
Title: Presto chango! : tricks for skilled magicians : 4D a magical augmented reading experience / by Norm Barnhart.
Description: Mankato, Minnesota : Capstone Press, 2018. | Series: Dabble lab.
   Amazing magic tricks 4D | Includes bibliographical references and index. |
   Audience: Age 8-12. | Audience: Grade 4 to 6.
Identifiers: LCCN 2017035464 (print) | LCCN 2017039150 (ebook) |
   ISBN 9781543505757 (eBook PDF) | ISBN 9781543505702 (library binding)
Subjects: LCSH: Magic tricks—Juvenile literature.
Classification: LCC GV1548 (ebook) | LCC GV1548 .B365 2018 (print) | DDC 793.8—dc23
LC record available at https://lccn.loc.gov/2017035464

. . . . . .

EDITOR:
Aaron J. Sautter

DESIGNER:
Ted Williams

PRODUCTION:
Katy LaVigne

. . . . . .

Image Credits
All photographs and video are done by Capstone Studio

Design Elements
Shutterstock: findracadabra, G.roman, javarman, popular business

Printed and bound in the USA.
010758S18

TABLE OF CONTENTS

INCREDIBLE MAGIC!

Magicians are storytellers. They weave wild tales about strange places and mysterious people while they perform their fantastic tricks. In these pages you'll learn several tricks to astound your family and friends. You can even add your own clever stories to keep your audience entertained. It's time to learn some incredible magic!

THE KEYS TO MAGIC

⭐ **Practice, practice, practice!** Try standing in front of a mirror while practicing with your props. Then you can see what the tricks look like to your audience.

⭐ **Keep it secret!** If you reveal the secrets of a trick, people won't be very impressed. It also ruins the trick for other magicians.

⭐ **Be entertaining!** Tell the audience jokes or stories while you do your tricks. It will keep them coming back for more.

A MAGIC SECRET — THE DITCH

The Ditch, or secret drop, is one of the most valuable secrets in magic. As you grab your magic wand, you secretly drop a hidden object into your magic trunk. Don't look stiff or nervous while you do this. Just act calm while you smoothly make the switch. The audience won't suspect a thing!

DOWNLOAD THE CAPSTONE 4D APP!

- Ask an adult to search in the Apple App Store or Google Play for "Capstone 4D".
- Click Install (Android) or Get, then Install (Apple).
- Open the app.
- Scan any of the following spreads with this icon:

When you scan a spread, you'll find fun extra stuff to go with this book! You can also find these things on the web at **www.capstone4D.com** using the password **magic.skilled**

MEET THE MAGICIAN!

Norm Barnhart is a professional comic magician who has entertained audiences for nearly 40 years. In 2007 Norm was named America's Funniest Magician by the Family Entertainers Workshop. Norm's travels have taken him across the United States and many countries around the world. He also loves to get kids excited about reading. Norm says, **"I love bringing smiles to people of all ages with magic. After reading this book, kids will love to do magic tricks too."**

THE MAGIC HANKY

Lots of people carry hankies in case they have to sneeze. Where do you think magicians keep their hankies? With this fun trick, you can make a colorful hanky appear from an empty paper bag!

WHAT YOU NEED

⭐ A colorful handkerchief
⭐ Two small paper bags
⭐ Colorful confetti

PREPARATION

1. For this trick, you'll need a secret pocket in the bottom of a paper bag. To make it, cut the top half off of one paper bag. Keep the bottom half for the next step.

2. Next, place the hanky at the bottom of the second bag. Then place the half bag inside the whole bag on top of the hanky. The hanky is now hidden inside the secret pocket. Now it's time to trick the audience!

MAGIC TIP

If you have a rainbow-colored hanky, have the audience pretend to take a tiny pinch of color off their shirts and toss it toward the bag. Then a rainbow-colored hanky amazingly appears!

1. First, tell the audience about your magic confetti that can create a new hanky any time you need one. Next, pick up the bag and show the audience that it's empty by turning it upside down. Ask a volunteer to stick a hand in the bag to make sure it's empty.

2. Now, toss some of the colorful confetti into the bag. Wave your wand over the bag and say a few magic words.

Next, blow the bag up like a balloon. Then twist the top and pop the bag so the confetti flies out as shown.

3. After startling the audience with the loud bang, it's time to amaze them by pulling out the colorful hanky. Say something like, "This magic confetti is great. It works every time!"

SEE HOW IT'S DONE

SUNDAY COMICS HERO

People love reading the Sunday comics pages. Everybody has a favorite character. You can make your favorite character appear out of nowhere with this fun trick!

WHAT YOU NEED

- ★ Colorful Sunday comics page
- ★ A small toy figure
- ★ Glue

PREPARATION

1. First, glue the comics together to make a secret, triangle-shaped pocket. Then glue the other edges of the paper together as shown. Be sure not to glue the opening of the pocket.

2. Next, hide the small toy figure inside the secret pocket. A thin, flat toy works best so the audience doesn't see that something is hidden inside.

MAGIC TIP

You can do this trick with a comic book too. Make a secret pocket by gluing a second back cover onto a comic book. Then just roll the comic book into a tube and let the toy slide out into your hand.

1. First, hold up the Sunday comics page and show it to the audience. Tell them a story about your favorite character. Mention how you love the character's adventures or how the character always makes you laugh. Be sure to keep the secret pocket hidden.

2. Tell the audience that the character sometimes likes to come out and say, "Hello." Then roll the paper into a cone shape so the secret pocket is in the middle. Next, wave your magic wand over the cone and say a few magic words.

3. Finally, reach into the cone and pull out the toy figure. Have the toy take a bow as the audience gives you a round of applause!

SEE HOW IT'S DONE

MAGIC MAG-NEE-TO MAN

Astonish your friends with your magical magnetic powers! Become the Magic Mag-Nee-To Man and make a plastic cup stick like a magnet to a book. It's an easy gravity-defying trick.

PREPARATION

1. First, bend one end of the paper clip so it sticks straight out. Then hold it against the book with your thumb as shown.

2. Now, place the cup over the paper clip and press it against the paper clip with your thumb. This is the secret of the trick. With enough practice, you'll be able to hold the book at any angle and the cup should stay in place.

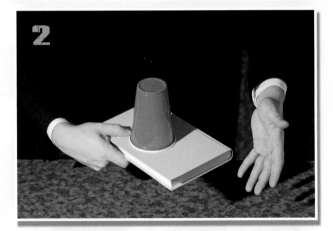

MAGIC TIP Try ending the trick by pretending that the cup is stuck to the book so well that you can't get it off. This will add some fun humor for the audience.

1. First, rub the cup against your hair. While you do this say, "People tell me I have a magnetic personality. And they're right. I can affect objects with my magnetic power!"

2. Now, get the book and paper clip from your magic trunk. Hold up the book and show it to the audience. Be sure they can't see that you're holding the paper clip behind the book. Then place the cup over the paper clip as shown.

3. Firmly hold the cup against the book like you practiced earlier. Then slowly turn the book over to show that the cup is stuck to it. Take a bow as the audience applauds your incredible magnetic abilities!

SEE HOW IT'S DONE

THE ESCAPING COIN

Big or small, all magic tricks are just illusions. Sometimes the best illusions are when the magic happens right in a person's hand. This one will leave the whole audience baffled!

WHAT YOU NEED

⭐ Seven coins

PERFORMANCE

1. First, tell the audience that money sometimes has a mind of its own and likes to escape. Pick up the coins one at a time and place them in your left hand. Count them out loud so the audience knows how many there are.

2. Now, ask a volunteer to hold out his or her hand. Count out loud as you transfer the coins, one at a time, from your hand into the volunteer's hand.

3. When you get to the sixth coin, tap it against the coins in the volunteer's hand as shown. The sound will cause the volunteer and the audience to believe that it landed with the other coins.

4. Instead of placing the sixth coin in the volunteer's hand, simply keep it hidden in your right hand as shown. This will take practice so the volunteer doesn't see that you keep it. Now, drop the seventh coin into the volunteer's hand. Ask your volunteer to close his or her hand tightly so no coins can escape.

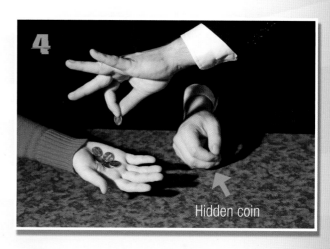

Hidden coin

5. Put your hand that is hiding the secret coin under the volunteer's hand as shown. Bump the volunteer's hand a couple of times, then let the hidden coin drop into your open left hand. Finally, ask the volunteer to count out the number of coins in his or her hand. When the volunteer counts only six coins, the audience will think the coin escaped right through the volunteer's closed hand!

SEE HOW IT'S DONE

THE ZOOMING MOON ROCK

Even rocks can get homesick. Here's a trick you can use to send a lonely moon rock zooming back home to the moon. Everybody will be left wondering how it's done!

WHAT YOU NEED

- ⭐ A small, shiny rock
- ⭐ Two foam cups
- ⭐ Scissors

PREPARATION

1. First, make a secret hole by cutting out the bottom of one foam cup with the scissors as shown.

2. Next, stack the cups so the cup with the secret hole is on the bottom. Then put the rock in the top cup as shown.

1. First, ask a volunteer in the audience to help you with this trick. Dump the moon rock into the volunteer's hand and ask him or her to show it to the audience. Then tell the audience a story about magical moon rocks that fly home to the moon when they get lonely.

2. Now, separate the cups. Be sure to hide the secret hole by keeping that cup in the palm of your hand as shown. Tell the audience that you're going to send the rock home with some help from your volunteer. Then have the volunteer put the rock back in the normal cup.

Secret hole

3. Next, place the two cups together mouth to mouth as shown.

4. Tip over the cups so the rock falls through the secret hole and into your hand. Be sure to keep the hole covered with your hand so the audience won't see it.

Hidden rock

5. Next, set the cups on the table so they are stacked mouth to mouth as shown. Be sure to keep the rock hidden in your hand.

6. Now, reach into your magic trunk with the hand holding the rock. Ditch the rock in the trunk and grab your magic wand.

7. Here's where the magic happens! Wave your magic wand over the stacked cups. You can ask your volunteer to repeat some magic words to help send the rock home too. Then pretend to watch the rock zoom home to the moon.

8. Finally, slam your hand down on the stacked cups to smash them up. Tear up the pieces to show that the rock has disappeared into outer space! Thank the volunteer and ask your audience to give him or her a round of applause!

MAGIC TIP Try having the volunteer wave the magic wand over the cups. He or she will be astounded that the rock disappeared!

SEE HOW IT'S DONE

THE TRICKY LEPRECHAUN

Leprechauns are real pranksters. The audience will be amazed when an invisible leprechaun steals a coin. Then they'll be surprised when you find it in a pot at the end of the rainbow!

WHAT YOU NEED

- Two identical coins
- A colorful handkerchief
- A shirt with a chest pocket
- A tissue
- A bowl

PREPARATION

1. First, place the two coins inside the bowl. Place the tissue into the bottom of your shirt pocket as shown. This helps keep the pocket open a bit.

PERFORMANCE

1. Pick up the bowl in one hand. As you do this, hide one coin behind your fingers. Then tip the bowl to drop the second coin into your other hand. Place the bowl on the table with the first coin hidden inside. Now, show the second coin to the audience and tell a story about a tricky leprechaun that likes to steal coins.

MAGIC TIP

Try hiding the secret coin in your shoe. When the coin disappears, pretend to feel something stuck in your shoe. Take your shoe off to reveal the hidden coin. The audience will get a good laugh from the leprechaun's trick!

2. Pick up the hanky and drag it over your hand and the coin. As you do this, grab the coin with your thumb and finger as shown. Be sure to keep the coin behind the hanky so the audience can't see it.

3. As you drag the hanky toward you, secretly drop the coin into your shirt pocket as shown. Be sure to keep your eyes on your empty hand under the hanky so the audience doesn't suspect anything.

4. Once the coin is hidden, pull away the hanky to show that the coin has disappeared! Act surprised at how fast that tricky Leprechaun is. Then start searching for the coin. Pretend to check your pockets and in your magic trunk. Finally, check the bowl on the table. The audience will be amazed at how the leprechaun hid the coin there!

SEE HOW IT'S DONE

MULTIPLYING MONEY

Everybody likes having plenty of money. Magic with money really grabs people's attention. This trick will make the audience wish their money could multiply this fast!

PREPARATION

1. First, create a secret pocket by taping the craft sticks to the bottom of the table as shown. The space between them should be a little smaller than the coins are wide. Be sure the pocket is near the side of the table you'll be sitting at.

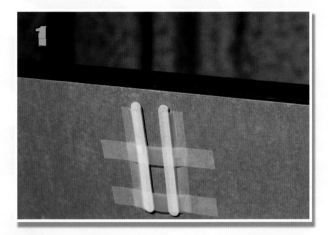

2. Next, slide two coins into the secret pocket. The gap between the sticks should allow you to easily get at the coins.

SEE HOW IT'S DONE

1. Start by laying out five coins on the table. Tell your audience, "Making money is easy. I can make these coins multiply." Ask a volunteer to count the coins on the table.

2. Now, slide the coins off the edge of the table with one hand so they drop into your other hand.

3. At the same time, use your second hand to slide the coins out of the secret pocket as shown.

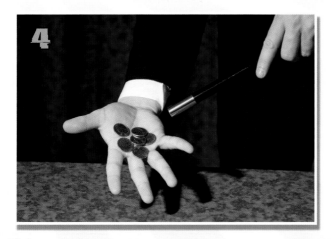

4. Close your hand around the coins. Then pretend to grab some invisible coins from the air and toss them into your hand. Wave your magic wand over your hand in a mystical way and say a few magic words. Finally, open your hand and have the volunteer recount the coins. The audience will be stunned when they see that the coins have multiplied!

THE MYSTIC SNOWFLAKE

No two snowflakes are exactly alike. With this trick you can make a paper snowflake with special magical scissors. The audience won't believe their eyes when it magically appears!

WHAT YOU NEED

- ✪ Two sheets of paper
- ✪ Scissors

PREPARATION

1. First, fold one sheet of paper in half three or four times. Then cut a few pieces out around the edges to make a paper snowflake.

Hidden snowflake

PERFORMANCE

1. Leave the paper snowflake folded up. When you're ready to do the trick, take the plain paper out of your magic trunk. At the same time, hide the paper snowflake in your hand as shown.

2. Tell the audience you can make a snowflake with magic invisible scissors. Show them the plain paper and fold it three or four times. With the final fold, secretly switch the plain paper with the snowflake. Hide the plain paper in the palm of your hand. Be sure the audience doesn't see you switch the two pieces of paper.

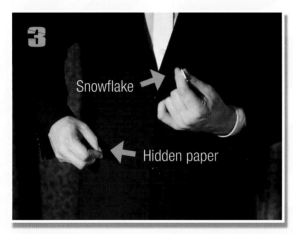

Snowflake

Hidden paper

3. Next, use the hand that is hiding the plain paper to reach into your pocket for your magic invisible scissors. Leave the paper behind in your pocket.

4. Now, pretend to pull out the magic invisible scissors. Use your fingers like scissors as shown, and pretend to cut out a paper snowflake.

5. Finally, unfold the paper snowflake and show it to the audience. They'll be amazed when they see that the paper has been transformed right before their eyes!

THE CRAZY COMICAL SOCK

The best way to warm up an audience is to get them laughing. With this trick, the audience gets a good laugh when you find something you didn't even know was lost!

WHAT YOU NEED

- Two identical socks
- A piece of black cloth
- A black hat
- Four safety pins

PREPARATION

1. First, pin or sew the black cloth into the bottom of the hat to create a secret pocket as shown. Then tuck a sock into the pocket.

2. Next, put the other sock on one foot. Leave your other foot bare inside your shoe as shown.

SEE HOW IT'S DONE

1. Start by telling the audience that you often find strange things in your hat. Tell them, "I never know what I might get when I do this trick." Then hold the hat up to show the audience that it's empty.

2. Now, wave your magic wand over the hat and say a few mysterious magic words.

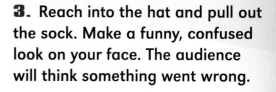

3. Reach into the hat and pull out the sock. Make a funny, confused look on your face. The audience will think something went wrong.

4. While looking confused, lift up your pant leg to show the matching sock that you're wearing. Then quickly lift your other pant leg to show that the sock is missing. Act surprised or embarrassed — as if you made the sock appear in the hat by mistake. The audience will have a good laugh and enjoy the rest of the show!

THE MAGIC PENNY BANK

Do you like saving your pennies? Now you can save money in a bottle without even removing the top. Your audience will be astounded when a coin seems to appear out of nowhere!

WHAT YOU NEED

- A plastic bottle
- 3 identical pennies
- A colorful handkerchief
- A needle and thread
- Tape

PREPARATION

1. First, place a small loop of tape inside the bottle's cap. Then lightly place one of the pennies on the tape as shown. Don't press the penny down too hard or the trick won't work.

2. Ask an adult to help you with this step. Hide a secret, second penny inside a secret pocket in the hanky. Do this by folding the corner of the hanky over the penny and sewing it in place as shown.

1. First, pick up the bottle and show the audience that it's empty. Tell them that you like saving your extra coins, but that you hate opening the top all the time. Then gently screw on the top. Be sure the hidden penny doesn't fall into the bottle.

2. Put the bottle down and pick up the third penny. Say, "I like saving my coins by magic instead." Then pretend to place the penny in the center of the hanky. Flip the hanky over, and casually bring the corners of the hanky, including the secret hidden penny, up to the middle of the hanky. As you do this, hide the third penny in the your other hand as shown.

Secret penny

Third penny

Secret penny

3. Now, ask a volunteer to hold the penny in the hanky. He or she will actually hold the secret penny hidden in the hanky. Be sure to keep the third penny hidden.

4. Get your magic wand out of your magic trunk. Secretly ditch the hidden third penny in the trunk as you pick up the wand. Or, you can pretend to reach into your pocket to get some magic dust and leave the penny behind in your pocket.

5. Next, wave your magic wand over the hanky and say a few magic words. Then quickly pull the hanky out of the volunteer's hand to show that the penny has vanished!

MAGIC TIP

You can make this trick even more amazing. Quickly pull the hanky from the volunteer's hand and bang it against the bottle to make the hidden penny drop. The audience will gasp when the penny instantly appears inside the bottle!

6. Now, pick up the bottle and cover it with the hanky. Give the magic wand to the volunteer and ask him or her to wave it over the bottle and say a few magic words. Then tap the bottle firmly against your hand. This should release the secret penny inside the bottle cap so it drops into the bottle. You should hear it rattle inside the bottle.

7. Finally, remove the hanky, open the bottle, and drop the penny into your volunteer's hand. The audience will be amazed at how the coin disappeared from the volunteer's hand and reappeared inside the bottle. Thank the volunteer for helping and ask the audience to give him or her a round of applause!

SEE HOW IT'S DONE

GLOSSARY

applause (uh-PLAWZ)—clapping hands to show appreciation or approval

audience (AW-dee-uhns)—people who watch or listen to a play, movie, or show

confetti (kuhn-FE-tee)—small pieces of colored paper that people throw at parties, parades, and other celebrations

ditch (DICH)—to secretly switch one object for another

gravity (GRAV-uh-tee)—a force that pulls objects together

humor (HYOO-mor)—the funny or amusing quality of something

illusion (i-LOO-zhuhn)—something that appears to be real but isn't

leprechaun (LEP-ruh-kawn)—a dwarf or elf in Irish folklore that likes to gather and hide treasure

magnetic (mag-NET-ik)—having the attractive properties of a magnet

prop (PROP)—an item used by an actor or performer during a show

trunk (TRUHNGK)—a large case or box used for storage or for carrying items

volunteer (vol-uhn-TIHR)—someone who offers to help perform a task during a show

READ MORE

Barnhart, Norm. *Fantastically Funny Tricks.* Magic Manuals. North Mankato, Minn.: Capstone Press, 2014.

Fullman, Joe. *The Great Big Book of Magic Tricks.* Laguna Hills, Calif.: QEB Publishing, 2014.

Turnbull, Stephanie. *Easy Dinner Table Tricks.* Beginner Magic. Mankato, Minn.: Smart Apple Media, 2014.

· · · · · ·

INTERNET SITES

Use FactHound to find Internet sites related to this book.

Visit www.facthound.com

Just type in 9781543505702 and go.

Super-cool stuff!

Check out projects, games and lots more at
www.capstonekids.com

INDEX